DARK HORSE

DARK HORSE

by John Fischer

MULTNOMAH PRESS
PORTLAND, OREGON 97266

Words from the song "Dark Horse," ©1982 by Word Music (a division of Word, Inc.). All rights reserved. International copyright secured. Used by permission. Words and music by John Fischer.

Cover art by Tom Williams

DARK HORSE
© 1983 by John Fischer
Published by Multnomah Press
Portland, Oregon 97266

Printed in the United States of America

First Printing 1983

Library of Congress Cataloging in Publication Data

Fischer, John.
   Dark horse.

   I. Title.
PS3556.I762D3   1983   813'.54   83-11411
ISBN 0-88070-016-5 (pbk.)

Dedicated

to
Christopher and Anne.
May they be dark horses running
into the next generation.

Foreword

Perhaps the most basic characteristic of fallen man is his inability to see himself in a true light. Personal blind spots afflict us all. We seem to see others clearly and are amazed at their blindness to themselves. But we are equally amazed at what they often see in us which we do not see!

It is this human quality which makes allegory helpful. Allegory is a way of seeing ourselves clearly (even our faults) precisely because it is not us that we are looking at. Ever since *Pilgrim's Progress*, the English-speaking world has been indebted to the allegorical method for spiritual insight and personal enlightenment.

In John Fisher's analogy of a horse that longed to be white, we shall all see the hidden hypocrisies that sabotage our dreams, but also those unexpected resources of the Spirit that can lead us to fulfillment.

The book is small but the theme is great. I hope you will enjoy both.

Ray C. Stedman

Preface

"Why don't you write a song about Ron?" she said one morning after breakfast. My wife often has song ideas for me. It's a hit and miss kind of thing. Her own identity is strong enough that she's not afraid to miss. This idea was definitely a hit, even though I fought it for a moment.

"I don't think it would work. Who would relate to a song about someone they didn't know?"

"They could relate to your relationship."

"Perhaps. No, I don't think it would work."

"I know," she said. "Make it allegorical. If Ron were an animal, what would he be?"

Pause.

"A stallion. An Italian stallion," I joked.

"That's been done."

"No. He would be a *black* stallion. A dark horse . . . that no one could ride. You know, I think you might have something here."

An hour later, the original song "Dark Horse" was born. It told about a man who showed me how to follow Christ through the power of the Holy Spirit.

Since its inception, the lyric has been changed to incorporate more than one specific person. The dark horse has become a symbol of the ordinary person who comes out a winner due to the grace of God. And the dark horse theme has become the rallying point for an album and now the inspiration for this book.

But most importantly, the dark horse is an image of real Christianity. Righteousness amidst human flaws.

The church is inundated with white horses. Flawless, successful, inaccessible leaders who only drive the average Christian deeper into frustration, guilt, and failure. If we are to learn to follow Christ, it will be the dark horses, not the white ones, that will show us the way.

John W. Fischer

He's a dark horse in the nighttime . . .

Night Flight

---

*F*or as long as I can remember, I had always wanted
to be a white horse. I wasn't all white, but my good
ancestry had left me more white than most horses I knew,
and fortunately, in the most important places. Most of
my face was white, and the white of my right front leg
ran up to my shoulder so that if I stood at an angle . . .
with my good leg out . . . and my head slightly cocked
. . . all you could see was white.

It was a good sign, I was told, and a mark of a leader.

It was for this reason that when I came of age, I was
sent to a special ranch where they trained horses like me
to think, walk, and prance like white horses. We learned
how to make the most of our white parts; even how to
pose so as to show the most amount of white (without
looking unnatural).

This was harder for some than others. I remember one
horse that had a beautiful white rump and tail and one
white streak between his eyes. His unfortunate fate was
always having to present himself backwards—not to men-
tion the strain on his neck from twisting over his shoulder
so that the white on his head could be seen.

Life at the white horse ranch was very ordered. We spent most every morning exercising on a track—our muscles had to be developed to their fullest for a more impressive display. Then, after a brief rest, we were washed, brushed, and groomed by our trainers for posing sessions.

Posing sessions were boring, but the preening and doting associated with them was something to which any horse could easily become accustomed. During these sessions, the owner of the ranch would often come by and comment on our progress. I was proud to be "one of the most promising animals he had seen in some time." (I often wonder now if he meant that, or if he told the same thing to all the horses simply to build up our horse pride.)

True or not, the words worked on me. I began to form quite an attachment to my own whiteness. I found myself more and more aware of it, almost as if it were glowing with a light of its own. But of course it was easy to become white-minded at a school where everything revolved around being white.

My favorite part of the day was after the posing sessions when we were led into a large pastured area, fed from long wooden troughs of hay, and allowed to run free in the late afternoon sun. During the spring there was even real grass to pull up with our teeth. I marveled at its sweetness and at the strange appeal of the gritty dirt in my mouth.

From the fenced pasture we would occasionally see small bands of wild horses moving across the plains in the distance. Seeing them always gave me a curious, restless sort of feeling. Like sniffing a spring wind that's blown across distant fields of clover. Almost in spite of myself I would move to the fence and watch them prance and canter on the horizon.

What would it be like to be . . . out there?

Part of me was drawn to the adventure, the freedom. But another part was full of questions. How would I be assured of food? Who would keep me clean? And—most important of all—what do they know of being white? What do they care? It was always this question that would shake me from such foal-ish daydreams and remind me that I was destined for a "higher calling." Whiteness could not be important out on the plains; it would be impossible to maintain. I was obviously dedicating myself to the true glory of horses—being white.

For this reason, the highlight of each year was when a white horse show came to our ranch. It was the one time we were able to see *real* white horses in all their splendor. Men would come to these shows in great numbers to see the bright spotlights reflect off these horses' magnificent heads, powdery white manes, and rippling, muscular flanks. I used to dream of being in that spotlight, because I knew that with its help, even though I wasn't, I could still look like a white horse. All of us at the ranch shared that one burning dream—to one day join a white horse show.

It was during one of these shows that I first met him. The shows always came during the first warm evenings of spring and this night was crystal clear, making the resplendent white horses appear unusually bright.

"Have you ever seen a white horse?"

The nicker came from behind me—so softly that only I could hear. I turned my neck to lay eyes on the most startling horse I had ever seen. Wild as a prairie storm. Dark as the night plains.

"Who are you—and how did you get in here?"

"I am not new to you."

Suddenly it came to me. He was the dark horse I had seen earlier outside the pasture fence. He had been the only wild horse to venture close to the ranch. Once he came near enough for me to strike up one of my more impressive, rehearsed poses. I had imagined this heathen horse would gasp with awe and gape in astonishment. But he didn't gasp or gape at all. He simply chewed on a mouthful of grass and looked me straight in the eyes. That look—I've never been able to erase it from my memory. It had a piercing clarity that seemed to burn even from a distance.

And now, up close, that look was making me very uncomfortable. It was as if he were looking right through my eyes into my very thoughts.

"Have you ever seen a white horse?" he repeated.

"Well of course. Isn't this a white horse show?"

"But have you ever *seen* a white horse?"

"I see the white horses that come in the show. And some of us here at the ranch are almost all white."

"Have you ever walked completely around a white horse?"

Now he was starting to rattle something in my thinking. True, I had only seen the real white horses from a distance. When they were through showing they were whisked away to the separate stables where they were always quartered. And then I thought of all the horses at the ranch, none of which were *all* white. I thought of all the horses I knew and had to admit, I had never walked completely around a white horse.

"Look at that horse right now in the spotlight," he said. "Do you see all of him?"

"No."

"Of course you don't. And watch—when he's through posing he'll walk off in the darkness. Do you see? The light only shines on the pose, not the real horse."

I was bewildered. Couldn't find the words for an answer. Who was this dark horse? Where had he come from?

Was he some kind of cynic? An enemy, perhaps, trying to discourage me from my calling? And how could one with no white on him seem to . . . well, *shine* the way he did?

I turned toward the stage. I had to find relief from this wild horse's scrutiny. I had to collect my thoughts. But as I stared at the staging area, something looked different. After looking at the dark horse, the stage lights looked— somehow lesser—more diffused. The light on the horses was a frothy glow, reflecting back a surface sheen . . . but the light in the eyes of the dark horse flashed with pinpoint clarity and burned deep as a branding iron. I watched the horses come and go in the spotlight, striking their poses with casual grace. They'd all been through this many, many times before.

Suddenly it all seemed so hollow. Useless. Lifeless.

And then with the new light that was already illumining my thoughts, I saw in an instant the folly of this whole procedure. How foolish that it had never occurred to me before! I wasn't going to get any whiter by being at this ranch—*only more clever at appearing white!*

I looked back again at the dark horse and his eyes were dancing with excitement. He knew what I was going through. Without even speaking he was willing me to ask the ultimate question. But who could ask such a question? To speak those words would be . . . horrifying. It would undermine everything I'd ever learned about the glory and purpose of horses. It would alter the whole course of my life. But it was no use holding back. The question had already asked itself in my mind and there was nothing that could keep it from falling out of my mouth.

"Do you mean to tell me . . . there are no white horses?"

"No," he replied. "There is one."

"You mean the White One?"

"Of course. He is the only white horse there ever was or ever will be."

"Aren't we to be like the White One?" It was another horse from the ranch speaking, for there was now a small group listening in on our conversation.

"Yes," said the dark horse. "But whiteness is not on the outside. It is in the heart. White isn't what you look like, it's what you do when you follow the will of the White One. You cannot change a hair on your body, but he can change your heart and shine his light in your eyes."

As I stood there the whiteness on my leg and face began to tingle as if it were glowing—not in a good way this time, but in an embarrassing way. Suddenly it seemed like a thousand eyes were focused on that small area of whiteness I had cherished for so long. How insignificant it became. I wanted to hide. The whiteness had been the focus of my trust, not the White One. I was ashamed.

I asked another question, trying to get the attention off myself for a moment. "Why then do we have white horse shows?" I asked. "What's the point?"

"That's the point . . . there *is* no point."

He was becoming restless as if my question had finally brought our discussion to the conclusion he was seeking. He pawed the ground, tossing his great head up and down with anger.

"There are thousands of horses out there who have never heard of the White One and there is an enemy afoot—crouching at the door—while you waste your time comparing whiteness."

At that he reared back and his cry was a mighty thing. *"If you would follow the White One, then follow me!"*

Just that quickly he was gone—vaulting two fences and galloping hard toward the open plains.

There was now no small commotion created in the white horse show. The air was choked with dust. Horses panicked and whinnied—people panicked and cried. The thunder of the bolting dark horse seemed to echo and re-echo from the stable walls as the spotlights turned off their subjects to search the crowd for the cause of the disruption. And the few of us who had heard the words were stamping our hooves in an agony of indecision. Even as I watched, the eyes of two of my companions began to flicker and flame. And in that instant I knew. It should have been a hard decision. But it was not. The truth was too clear. The challenge was too compelling. The alternative was too costly. There was a choice, but there was no choice.

The next events happened so fast that I only remember flashes and pictures. But those pictures will always stay vivid in my mind. The flying dust, the easily-vaulted fences, the pounding hooves, the sweat and dirt mingling to mud and caking on my white leg, the faint outline of the other horses—black against the night sky.

Racing into the darkness, we had only the stars for light. That, and the light of the White One, shining through our eyes, driving us across plains we had never run, towards mountains we had never seen.

Headin' straight for the enemy camp . . .

Warnings

We galloped all night until a fringe of orange-red light began to outline the mountains, still far in the distance. I had never run so far and so fast. And as we grazed and watered in the cool freshness of the morning, an intense pain crept into my limbs. The exhilaration of our night flight had numbed my senses, but as the excitement wore off, the real cost to my untried muscles was making itself painfully known.

There were five of us now—four plus the dark horse. Two of the horses were from the ranch, but the other one was unfamiliar to me. He had a stronger odor than the horses I was used to, and his coat was thickly matted. He'd never been groomed. It was obvious he had spent his whole life on the plains.

Normally I would have been intimidated by such a horse. One glance at my once-white leg, however, reminded me that I wasn't quite the tame horse that *I* had been just a few hours earlier.

"You run well," the plains horse said to me.

I was honored, but I had to reply honestly. "I *ran* well. Right now I feel like I'll never run again."

"You are not used to the plains?"

"Listen, I'm not used to being outside of a fence! The only running I'd done before last night had been in circles."

The plains horse thought about that for a moment.

"Don't feel so bad," he said. "I've been running in circles most of my life, too. Does that surprise you? I can see that it does. Well let me tell you, some of us who wander create our own fences. And imaginary fences are as confining as real ones. That's why I decided to join up with the dark horse. He runs straight. He knows where he's going and there's always light in his eyes."

"Where *are* we going?"

The question came from one of the ranch horses who'd been listening in on our conversation. With one accord, the three of us trotted over to where the dark horse was standing on a low bluff overlooking the shallow river where we had stopped for water.

We were still on the plains. The ground was red in the morning sun and there wasn't a tree in sight. The only thing you could see for miles was the low-lying scrub brush hugging the dry, sandy soil. Our lead horse was standing on the very edge of the bluff, ears pricked straight up, and staring into the distance as if he could hear or see something far ahead. I looked too, for a moment, but saw only a gently rolling terrain that marked the beginning of the foothills.

This time I asked the question.

"Where are we going?"

Instead of replying, the dark horse waited for the fifth stallion to finish his drink at the river and join us. It was clear he wanted us all together before he spoke.

"We are going towards the enemy camp," he finally answered.

"How far is it to the enemy camp?" asked one of the

schooled horses.

"As far as it will always be if we keep moving."

We were quiet for a few moments, acting like we understood when we didn't. The plains horse finally spoke up.

"I don't understand."

"As long as you run *towards* the enemy camp," said the dark horse, "you will never reach it."

"You mean, we don't *want* to get there?" I asked, puzzled.

"Precisely."

Now what kind of donkey-talk was that? I'd run all night long pursuing a target I didn't want to reach? Suddenly I found myself thinking about the white horse ranch—my hay-carpeted stall, hot mash for breakfast, the attention, the routine, the grooming. Ah me, wouldn't a rub down feel good right now! Then the thought hit me—a cold jolt in my tired bones. *There was no going back.* I had left the white horse ranch for good. I couldn't find it now even if I wanted to turn around. This wasn't just a lark—a trot down the road that would be over tomorrow. I was standing tired and muddy in a strange land following a strange horse who spoke strange words and pursued a strange destination we didn't want to reach! I felt very alone.

Then the plains horse broke in on my thoughts.

"I don't understand," he said.

Good ol' plains horse! I was already starting to like him. He would be the one who would say what we were all thinking.

"The enemy dwells in darkness," said the dark horse. "He thrives in it. He can only do his work in the dark. If we run *towards* him he must flee from us—we have the light of the White One in our eyes and he can't bear it. But if we stay in one place, we begin to doubt whether there is an enemy at all. Then as we take our ease and enjoy our comforts, he moves his camp closer and closer to ours until he is able to influence us without our even knowing it."

I immediately thought of the jealousy and strife that went on at the white horse ranch. Could that have been caused by the "influence" he was talking about? And then there was the deception of always trying to appear white. Dishonesty. Even then I was beginning to recognize it as one of the enemy's favorite weapons. It keeps us from knowing the power of the White One himself.

"So we just keep moving—constantly?" asked the plains horse.

"No. There is a season for everything. But even when we rest someone must stand guard. It's in times of ease when we are most susceptible to the enemy's devices."

"Is the enemy the only reason we keep moving?" I asked.

The dark horse paused a moment before he spoke. "Look ahead and tell me what you see."

"Foothills."

"And beyond that?"

"Mountains."

"And beyond that?" There was a longer pause. "And beyond that?" he repeated.

"We don't know," said the plains horse.

The dark horse, who had been staring all this time out towards the mountains, turned and looked us each in the eye.

"Do you want to know?"

"Yes!" we cried in unison.

"Then that is why we go."

A shiver of excitement swept through me from muzzle to tail. For the first time I felt a sense of challenge—not fear—at the gate of the unknown.

"How do you know the way?" asked one of the ranch horses. "There is no path."

The dark horse was very patient with our questions. In fact, he seemed eager to answer. We would realize later that this question and answer process would be our main source of learning. "Teachable moments," he would call them.

"There is a path," he said, "but it is known only to the White One. He reveals it as we go. You cannot see where it leads—only where to take the next step."

There was a lull in the questioning. The sun was quickly shooing away the early morning chill and its sleepy warmth had a couple of us slipping into a drowse. What a great relief when the dark horse announced we were to sleep! He gave the plains horse the first watch since he was the least tired.

"We will travel again at the rising of the moon," he said.

Sleep mounted my shoulders like an impatient rider, eager to gallop into sweet oblivion. But for a moment I fought it off. The plains horse had asked another question and I wanted to hear the answer.

By now the voice of the dark horse seemed to be coming from the sun, bathing my mind as the warmth seeped into my weary muscles.

"We travel at night," said the voice, "because this is the age of darkness. Darkness is the reality . . . daylight is the lie. Run in the daylight and you'll be fooled by a lesser light or a well-worn path. He would lead us along new paths . . . paths to be found at night, for then we see only what he reveals to us. A morning comes when his light will ride the plains of the sky—the beginning of eternal day. But until that morning we run at night, because it is truly night in the world . . ."

His last words trailed off into my dreams. Like fading

hoofbeats. Too exhausted for deep sleep, I dreamed most of the day. Not about mountains. Not about adventures and night rides. But about the white horse ranch, my comfortable stall . . . and the fading comfort of my once white leg.

And he has no fear 'cause his eye is clear . . .

Trapped

As I awoke the fresh hay in my stall slowly vanished into hard ground. The roof of my stall faded into a wide sky. Reality rudely pushed aside the white horse ranch, and reality was painful.

But even in those first moments of waking, I could sense a tingling something under the pain. Adventure! And the first adventure was simply getting onto my feet. My legs felt like foolish, useless things—hardly attached to my body.

I must have looked silly sitting there on my rump with my rigid forelegs stretched in front of me, searching for enough courage to rise. I felt humiliated. But even worse, I had a strong premonition that this was only the first of many humiliating positions in this new way of life. Hunching my back, I finally gave one great heave with my untried legs and, like a newborn colt getting up for the first time, I accomplished the initial task of the evening.

Hello, new world.

And it really was a new world. As the events of the previous night slowly returned to my mind, I was aware of a new feeling. Not the longing for what I had left behind, but the excitement and anticipation of what lay ahead.

My body was tired, but my spirit seemed charged with a freshness that made me wonder if I'd ever been alive before. I had fallen asleep wanting to go back. No longer. A miracle had worked its work inside me, borne on the long wind of a prairie afternoon. Now nothing could keep me from attacking those new horizons—no matter what the cost. (Good thing, too. In my present condition it cost to move at all.) Months later I would reflect on that first afternoon and realize a miracle *had* taken place, for I never again felt a desire to turn back.

I looked over at my three sleeping trail-mates. It made an eerie picture. They were sprawled out on the ground, bathed in the blood-red glow of the setting sun. A passing stranger might have thought he'd stumbled on the aftermath of some great battle. If it hadn't been for the loud, contented snoring, it might have made a convincing picture.

I found the dark horse standing straight and alert at the ragged edge of the rocky bluff. He had taken over the watch sometime during the day and now gazed out over the rolling foothills and the gathering dusk. He looked as if he'd been planted in that watchful position all day long. I was convinced that if he'd slept at all, it was only in a few brief dozes.

He turned to watch my approach. "First time on your feet?" he nickered, rolling his eyes. He was joking, of course, about my wobbly, foal-like walk. Well, let him joke. I was ready to run—even if my legs weren't.

"When do we set out?" I asked. His eyes danced. I could tell that my eagerness pleased him.

"Very soon," he replied. "But first you need a roll in the water. Do you good. There's a nice sandy spot over there where the river bends."

The river held the last red of the dying sun and as I plunged in, its icy current stung life back into my wooden limbs. I rolled and rolled in the shallows, surprised at how good the smooth stones felt on my back. It was like a new experience that should have been an old one. Being groomed by men was never as good as this.

By the time I was back on my feet the others had arrived and there was more than a little playful splashing going on. Suddenly I felt a nip at my hindquarters, just above the tail. I wheeled around to see the plains horse, looking as surprised as I was.

"What's the matter?" he said. "Haven't you ever been groomed by a horse?"

"Well, no. I've always been kept separate from the others. I've only been groomed by men."

"Well turn around, friend. I've got a treat for you." With that he started nipping and pulling and biting the hair all over my back and neck. It was rougher treatment than I had ever known, but somehow . . . it felt right. Soon we were all nipping at each other's backs. A few bites landed harder than some, and it wasn't long before the whole scene turned into a playful battlefield.

The dark horse himself took part in the fray. But not by choice—and not for long. Intimidated by no one, the plains horse came alongside our leader and nipped him on the flank. But instead of nipping back, as the game usually goes, the dark horse twisted violently away and half reared, pawing the water. Taking this as a mock challenge, the rest of us surrounded him and began to close in, delighted that he would allow us to spar with him.

But we took him wrong. And he wasn't sparring.

Shaking his mane, the dark horse lunged and kicked and the blows weren't playful. Not at all.

We stopped our attack, of course, and a long moment

of embarrassing stillness followed as we stood frozen in the water.

"We will run again at the rising of the moon," he said. Without a further word or glance he trotted back to his lookout on the bluff. We stood there in the river, dripping wet, feeling like fools.

"What was all *that* about?" murmured one of the schooled horses.

"I can't imagine," said the other. "But really—I'm shocked at such behavior . . . and coming from *him.*"

"I'm relieved," said the plains horse. We looked at him. "I was beginning to wonder if he was a real horse—or something beyond our reach." He glanced up at the bluff.

"He's real all right."

He had a point. I had to admit, even though I was smarting from one of his blows, that I felt closer to the dark horse now. His vulnerability made him . . . well, more believable. Somehow the power of the White One now seemed more accessible—to all of us. If the dark horse had room to grow, there was hope for me, too.

A little later, as I stood dozing after an adequate meal, I felt a surge of kinship for our little band—all of them. Apparently my "afternoon miracle" wasn't mine alone. We stood there together feeling the wind in our manes, silently waiting for the first glow of the moon to turn the chattering river into a broad silver road. We all knew it without saying: The night was cool, the night was sweet.

And we were ready to run.

The first few hours of travel were relatively easy. We were in the foothills now and every gradual rise seemed to peak at just the right time for a reviving downhill lope. It wasn't until we reached a high plateau that I realized how many more ups there had been than downs. We had actually climbed to a much higher plain.

I was pleasantly surprised at being able to keep up with the others. It was definitely painful, but it was a good pain—like growing pains. I knew I was becoming stronger. And the night was so glorious that even if I had wanted, I couldn't have focused on my pain for more than a moment. The air was crisp and cool, the ground was just hard enough to make a horse feel like flying, and the moon was so clear that it appeared to be resting on the crest of each new hill. Once I glimpsed the dark horse silhouetted in the center of that moon, as if one grand leap would send him flying into it, tearing it away from its moorings in the sky.

"Which way . . . do we go now?" someone panted.

"Down," said the dark horse. "But we must feed, water . . . and take a brief rest . . . before we begin again. It may be . . . some time before we . . . reach another place to stop."

We were standing, our backs steaming, at the edge of a deep, narrow canyon. Strong gusts of wind blew up over the lip where we stood, throwing hair back and forth across my eyes. There was the faint roar of rushing water below. The moon, at our backs, threw its silvery light halfway down the opposite canyon wall. The descent before us, however, was cloaked in shadow. I could see my hooves, the rim of the plateau where we stood, and then total blackness.

"We're going *down there?*"

"That's what the horse said."

It was the longest night I have ever spent. We descended single file, behind the dark horse, our noses pressed against the tail of the horse in front of us. It reminded me a little of the "close order" drills at the white horse ranch where one of us would prance behind the other in perfect step at a distance of just one pace.

But this was no drill. The loose shale was no carefully-manicured practice lawn. And we were anything but in step. Time and time again someone would slip, forcing our little party to slide into each other until we all regained our footing, sending a cascade of shale into the river far below. In this manner, by taking two steps and slip-sliding three, we picked our way into the night.

The mounting rumble of the water below was as gradual as the approach of dawn. By the time I could make out the silhouette of the rump in front of me, we had reached the river, and the roar was so loud we could not hear each other speak.

Dawn revealed the dramatic landforms that had turned our moonlight canter into a groping crawl. We had descended a virtual crack in the ground—a thin gorge that was still only wide enough at its floor to channel the rushing river that had created it.

The dark horse's first attempt was to lead us downstream, where there appeared to be slightly more room to pass along the river bank. That attempt, however, soon proved futile. Not far downstream the river made a flying leap into still another, deeper gorge. We had no choice but to reverse our direction and head upstream. Reversing our direction also reversed our order, putting me in the lead—a most inadequate, fearful leader, I thought.

When we reached the spot where we turned downstream I stopped and looked longingly up at the steep canyon wall we had descended during the night. I knew it would be impossible to climb back up the loose shale, but somehow going back seemed preferable to contending with a screaming river that clawed with frothy talons at the rocks and canyon walls.

But the dark horse would have none of that. Splashing through the dangerous shallow white water at the river's edge, he overtook the lead (to my relief) and struck out upstream.

And so upstream it was. Sometimes at river level, sometimes higher on impossible rocky shelves when the water challenged both sides of the gorge.

It must have been mid-morning by then, but who could tell in this deep, sunless canyon? Two colors dominated everything—black and gray. And those colors were close to the two feelings in my heart as we staggered along the rocky bank. One was a feeling of being pinched by the towering walls. It was as if we had fallen into some yawning chasm in the earth's surface that at any moment might decide to close up and swallow us whole. The other was a feeling of foreboding. The river rushed headlong to the precipice downstream, preferring to choose its own death rather than face what it had seen further up. My horse sense tugged at me with invisible reins to join the river in its flight—to flee the unknown terrors upstream.

These dark feelings were short-lived, however, for it wasn't long until we could see a thin, vertical slit of sunlight ahead. Hunger for the open spaces made us tremble and quicken our pace. Then, as that ribbon of light began to widen, we lost all sense of caution. Racing down the embankment or splashing through the rough stones on the river's edge, the five of us exploded into the dazzling sunlight at a full gallop.

One by one we made our grand entry into that arena of light, furiously twisting and turning, leaning our bodies first this way and then that, and tossing our heads up and down as if to cast off a hated rider.

Have you ever watched birds soar and wondered if they do it just for fun? Have you ever heard a coyote howl and wondered if he does it just to feel the lonely night shudder at his ghostly shrill? Have you ever caught a glimpse of horses with their ears laid back in full gallop and wondered if they do it just to hear their hooves beat the ground and echo back off canyon walls like a thousand pounding drums?

We do. And I had just found out.

I frolicked until I had exhausted my pent-up energy and gotten myself thoroughly separated from the other horses. Scattered whinnies around the valley told me the others had done the same. We'd had enough of single file. My new-found freedom was already convincing me: Horses were never meant to go single file.

As we slowly made our reunion I surveyed this sun-splashed valley that had caused such an abrupt change in our spirits. The once-ominous cliffs were now far apart, merely a dark backdrop for thickening stands of green aspen. The river, too, was transformed. In place of the raging tyrant, two harmless streams flowed at the foot of the cliffs on either side of the valley. While the trees followed the water, hugging the canyon walls, the center of the valley was treeless, covered with knee-high grass that was already turning late-spring yellow.

Our small group reassembled near one of the valley walls, where we all plunged our muzzles into the clear cold water of the stream. All of us, that is, except the dark horse. No one was particularly concerned about his absence at the time. He had frequently trotted on ahead of us, scouting out the best way.

"No doubt he's planning our next night run," said one of the schooled horses.

"I'd just as soon stay here a few days," I said. Fatigue was settling in again. The warm midday sun was tonic for our weary muscles.

As we grazed, I couldn't help reflecting on the shocking changes that had occurred in my life in such a brief time—and how long that "brief time" seemed! Two suns that felt like a lifetime. Within that time I had done what I thought impossible—certainly impossible for *me!* Other stronger, wilder horses might attempt such things, but me? Ridiculous! My mind clicked off the absurdities, one by one: *Escaped the white horse ranch. Vaulted two fences. Galloped all night. Galloped a second night on sore muscles. Descended a steep canyon wall at midnight. Ran like a carefree foal along the very edge of a death-dealing torrent.* I had actually done these things! Me! The same horse that scarcely two suns ago had been content with a small stall, a daily grooming, and a bale of hay. And here I was tearing up sweet grass from rich earth in the middle of an unknown canyon. And dearly loving it. Perhaps this was what it meant to be a real white horse.

"White isn't what you look like," the dark horse had said, "it's what you do when you follow the will of the White One."

After a full meal we discussed what we should do next. The plains horse wanted to canter on ahead and catch up with the dark horse, who was probably further up the valley. But the rest of us felt he knew where we were and would come back for us. Better to stay put than move and make it harder for him to find us. Besides, the midday sun, our full stomachs, and the long night were combining to make us all very drowsy. We tried to stand and doze, which would have kept us more alert to danger, but one by one we dropped to our knees and rolled over on our sides. We succumbed to the peaceful buzzing of bees in the clover, a caressing breeze that rippled the grass, and the warm, warm sunlight.

Soon I was racing back through the gorge—not on the rocky banks but thundering through the middle of the river, sending up great showers of spray in every direction. Coming to the waterfall I leaped into the air and soared like a falcon—over the canyon and far, far over the plateau and across the foothills until I could see the tiny whitewashed buildings of the white horse ranch below.

Suddenly I was standing on stage with the spotlight blinding my eyes. Purposely showing my dark side, I started shouting, "No, no! You have it all wrong! White isn't what you look like, it's what you do when you follow the will of the White One!" And then there was a great confusion as the spotlights blinked out and horses and men rushed upon me, heaving me off stage. The dark horse himself stood at the bottom of the ramp, his eyes aflame in the night. "No one is standing guard!" he cried, and his voice was like a thundering river in a narrow canyon. He was angry, and smoke billowed through his flaring nostrils. Then smoke was in *my* nostrils and I began to choke and suddenly I wasn't dreaming and the smoke was everywhere.

A huge black cloud was billowing up from the ground, bearing down on us from the other end of the valley!

Now there is nothing more frightening to a horse than fire. He can scale heights, fight in wars, march through driving snow and rain, and cross virtually any terrain, but put fire before his eyes or the smell of smoke in his nostrils and even the wisest horse dissolves into raving madness. He will kick down a stall, trample anything in his way, and even plunge over a cliff to his death without stopping to think about it.

Now this very terror was upon us. In an instant we were reduced to mindless running things. Just four legs and a wild fear.

In my confusion, I first ran directly for the fire. A strong wind, however, was herding it and us back towards the narrow mouth through which we had entered. The flames were sweeping the entire width of the valley. In the middle, the grass was burning low and even. But at the valley rim, the timber fed the fire into an inferno. Great sheets of flame leaped from the treetops, blackening the rock walls.

We would have trampled him—but for the fire in his eyes. Fire which flared hotter than the one from which we ran. The dark horse stood like a terrible sentinel, guarding our only exit from the burning valley—the familiar dark gorge where the two peaceful streams came together and began their wild canyon plunge. It was the only way in the world he could have captured our attention—and he did so at great risk. We were stampeding, funneled to the gorge opening by the canyon walls. We reached the spot where he stood at the same time with the same conclusion: We were trapped!

"If you had left a horse on guard, you would have discovered the fire before it crossed the entire valley!" The dark horse was screaming over the roar of both fire and water. "Now we are boxed in."

"Then we'll go back!" cried the plains horse.

"No!" said the dark horse, rolling his eyes and pursing his lips. "The White One *never* leads us back, only forward."

"But that's impossible! Forward is into the fire!"

"Then we go into the fire."

"But we'll perish," I cried.

"That is for him to decide. If he wants us to live, he will provide a way."

There was a moment of thought that seemed forever. *Through the fire?* How could I possibly do that? Deny my instincts, my fears, my very nature? Who was this dark horse and his White One that would lead us to our death? The voice of the dark horse broke suddenly into my thoughts.

"Now! There is no more time! If you would follow the White One, follow me!" And he was off. Into the fire.

I stood frozen for an instant. Watching him disappear into the smoke, I suddenly recalled how he had led me out of the white horse ranch into freedom and beauty and adventure. It was the same now, except he was leading me into fire and death. Could this too be the way of the White One?

I found myself running—running hard in the path of the dark horse. But it was like running through a hedge of thorns. Something was tearing at me, straining within me, fighting and warring with my nature. Then, with a great rending that seemed to rip through my whole being, I leapt into the flames on the flying hooves of the dark horse.

Every time I threw my legs forward it was pain. But this pain had nothing to do with resistant muscles—this was the pain of a resistant will. I was constantly fighting an overpowering influence to turn back—to save my life. It was like a choking bit in my mouth and slashing spurs in my sides. Everything in me told me I shouldn't be doing this. Everything but a new voice that sang encouragement to my spirit and urged me forward. And even as I listened, the voice sang louder. It was pure and clear and strong and bright. And it was winning.

Smoke clawed at my eyes. Hot gases seared my nostrils and tore at my heaving lungs. I closed my eyes and kept running against all reason. Or was I running at all? It felt like I was swimming—upstream—in a river of living flame.

How long would the fire burn? Could I run fast enough to survive?

Suddenly I was aware of a word. It wasn't a voice speaking, just an impression coming from deep within me—from the same place where the new impulse had driven me to follow the dark horse into this storm of fire.

Water.

Of course. The stream!

Turning in the direction where I thought the nearest

canyon wall would be, I ran with everything I had left. Scant seconds before I would have passed out, I found myself falling into the stream like a flying ball of flame. It was a fall that helped to save me. The stream was shallow, but as I hit the water I rolled completely over, dousing any attempt of the fire to burn my skin.

I now knew that the water would be my salvation—I wasn't going to die. But I had to find a deeper spot. Rising on miraculously uninjured legs, I splashed my way upstream.

The flames from the trees on either side joined above me, turning my waterpath into a fire-tunnel. Even though I was up to my belly in the stream, the heat was still unbearable. I had to get lower in the water. Somehow my strength held out until I reached a deep pool where with one last desperate plunge, I was completely immersed in the cool water.

Horses are buoyant. Swimming is easy. And as I waited out the fire, my only remaining worry was the flaming debris from the trees above.

It was a slow, thorough fire. The flames seemed deliberate. Almost painstaking in their efforts to spare no living thing. Still, I was spared. And so was a small patch of grass along the river bank on which I threw myself into a long, exhausted sleep.

And maybe sometime at the right time
You may see him gallopin' by . . .

Another Dark Horse

I felt her presence before I ever opened my eyes.
She was vigorously cropping the grass near where I
lay. That didn't make much horse sense. No mare in her
right mind would graze so close to a strange, sleeping
stallion. She must have been *very* hungry.

Quickly checking the position of the sun, I shut my
eyes and tried to remember what had happened to me. It
was midmorning. So I must have been asleep all night.

Then it came back to me. The fire. The stream. Escape.

Was I burned? Injured? Mentally, I felt over my whole
body and sensed no sign of serious burn. Then I began
twitching my muscles. They were sore, of course, but
seemed to be in proper working order.

I had made it, then. I had made it through the fire. But
what about the other horses? Had they survived too?
And then there was this mare. Surely she had not come
into this valley by the way we had entered. Perhaps there
was another entrance. But if that was true, why hadn't
she fled the fire?

I opened my eyes again and this time she jumped back
a few steps. She had seen me twitch and knew I was wak-

ing up.

"Are you all right?" she asked.

"I think so . . . but I won't know for sure until I stand up."

She was beautiful. Her coat was an amber that appeared more red in the sunlight than it did brown. She had a white streak between her eyes and white on her forelegs up to the knees. And she seemed spirited. Not like the shy mares I knew at the white horse ranch. I immediately liked the way she held her head high when she spoke. She came on like a stallion, but her features and movements were more graceful than any mare I had ever seen.

"Well," she said, "why don't you *try* getting up?"

"I will if you'll give me half a chance. Hmm. Thanks, by the way, for leaving me some grass to eat." I struggled into an upright position, trying hard to retain some dignity.

"I left you the grass where you were lying."

"Thanks." I wondered if she would have moved me if I had slept any longer. Actually, I was more thirsty than hungry. I turned to look for a drinking spot in the stream. It wasn't easy. The current was still choked with ash and charred debris from the fire.

I returned from my drink to find her finishing up the grass that I matted in my sleep.

"Sorry," she said, "but we haven't eaten for two days."

"There are more of you?"

"Oh yes. There are at least twelve of us who survived the fire."

"How did you get in here?"

"I should be asking *you* that," she said. "I've been here all my life and the herd has been here for generations. Where did you come from and how did you get through the fire?"

"I'll answer that another time," I said, putting her off.

"First you must take me to the others."

"They're all scavenging for food just like I am. But we have a meeting place for midday. If we leave now we should be there at the right time. Come with me."

As we walked, I questioned her about the herd. Apparently they had lived in the valley for so long that no one knew for sure how they had gotten there. The stories that had been passed down were a hopeless confusion of fact and legend. Although there were different schools of belief, none could actually prove their version of the story. The mare had her own belief: *None* of them were right.

However they had gotten in, they were all agreed on one thing: They would never get out. Strong Black Magic surrounded the only two possible escape routes. One such route was called the "Cavern of Thunder." The way our party had come in. The other route, at the opposite end of the canyon, was known as the "Death Walk." A few had tried the latter escape within the mare's lifetime. Each had met with a horrible death.

Obviously familiar with the "Cavern of Thunder," I questioned her carefully about the "Death Walk." I suddenly felt a strong desire to know as much as I could about the valley and its possible escape routes. Almost as if I were on some kind of assignment to lead the valley horses out. Perhaps I was.

"The Cavern of Thunder is at one end of the valley. At the other end, the walls meet again where the river falls into the valley."

"But what about the Death Walk?" I asked.

"I'm getting to that. The Death Walk is a ledge which runs up the rock wall by the falls. No one really knows whether it reaches the top, because all who have tried end up on the valley floor. Their bones are a constant reminder that we are trapped here forever."

"You believe this Black Magic, don't you?"

"Yes, I do."

"But what does my being here say about that magic?"

"I've been thinking about that. You must either be a part of the magic or . . . stronger."

"What do you think?" It suddenly seemed important to know how she perceived me.

"I don't know," she replied. "But . . . there's something about your eyes that makes me feel safe."

My heart pranced at her words. And it was just then that we came upon the other horses, gathered at the foot of the canyon wall across the stream at the opposite end of the valley. As we splashed through the stream, the others looked up and realized I was a new horse. I could see them freeze in position—ears pricked straight up. The first one to move was the stallion I took to be the leader. Driven by ancient instincts, he arched his neck and began a ritual of threat-display common to all lead stallions when challenged by an intruder—especially in the presence of mares. I complied with the ceremony, but the crisis of the situation we were in made it all seem so foolish. When he was finally convinced I had no intention of challenging his leadership, we were able to talk. The other horses, who had remained aloof during our sparring, came closer. Sniffing my breath, their faces were full of curiosity.

"How did you come into the valley?" asked the leader.

"Through the Cavern of Thunder," I said, using my local knowledge to good effect. Some of the horses took a step back.

"How did you survive the fire?"

"Through the water. I found refuge in a deep pool in the stream."

He nodded thoughtfully, obviously impressed. For a moment I struggled with the desire to keep him impressed, but then I knew I would never be comfortable taking credit where it wasn't due.

"I was led there by the White One."

"Who?"

"The White One."

"Where is this 'White One' and why is he not with you?"

"He *is* with me. He is within me."

I watched the puzzled look on his face and realized how little sense this all must make to him. A horse breaks the Black Magic and enters their valley, talking about being led by some white horse inside of him.

The answer, I realized, was to tell them all the story of the White One. As I spoke, I noticed the faces of my listeners. Most of them had the same curious look. The lead stallion was stoic, but the mare was the most enthusiastic. I couldn't be sure, but for a moment it seemed like I caught a slight glint of light flickering in her eyes.

I also noticed—in amazement—my own growing excitement in an old truth. I had known the story of the White One, of course, since I was a colt and had recited it countless times at the white horse ranch. But now I was *living* it! And just that suddenly I realized why I had come to this valley and what I was supposed to do.

"For centuries now the White One has been freeing horses from all kinds of captivity. This valley has been your captive place for generations. Until now, you haven't minded. It was beautiful and it provided for your needs. But now you see it for what it is—a charred, boxed-in canyon with hardly enough life to support even one of you.

"Even if there had been no fire, I still would have encouraged you to leave this place. There is so much more to life than you have experienced here. Why, there are plains to roam . . . mountains to scale . . . valleys to discover and—countless other horses to set free. Beyond all that is the adventure of moving with the White One. Once you have his spirit within and his purpose driving you on, you realize you have never lived before."

I paused, seeking to gather words for a final statement. One part of me was listening to myself in utter wonder. I had never spoken such words before. And the feeling in my heart flowed like a bottomless spring.

"I plead with you . . . come with me. There is only death left in this place. I know the White One will lead us out, because I know now that is why he brought me here . . . to you. I stand before you now as living proof that he is stronger than any Black Magic."

We stood still for a moment, the smell of smoldering death in our nostrils. It seemed so obvious to me. Even without the White One, I would prefer to die trying to escape rather than die in a burned out valley.

The mare spoke, breaking the stillness. "I remember a legend my father used to tell . . . about a dark horse that freed us from a great calamity. Perhaps . . . perhaps it wasn't a legend at all, but a prophecy of this very moment."

"Dark horse, white horse, legend, prophecy," said the stallion, restlessly stamping his hooves. "This is beyond me. We must take counsel among ourselves on this matter. We will meet you here tomorrow at midday."

"No," I said. "I leave at moonrise. Whoever would come with me has until sunset to decide."

"You travel at night?" said the stallion. "Now I know you are mad."

"I know it is hard for you to understand," I said, trying to brush aside his insult, "but the light the White One gives us is truer than the light of day. I will leave you to your discussions and return at sunset for any who wish to come with me." At that I turned, dashing across the stream and galloping towards the end of the canyon that

I had not yet seen.

Since I was so unfamiliar with the upper part of the canyon, I thought it best to take the rest of the day to investigate. The ground was warm from the fire, and wisps of smoke still rose from the valley floor as if escaping from yet another fire, deep in the entrails of the earth. I stopped further up, where the stream ran clearer, and took long drinks and a roll in the freezing water. The spring thaw was still working high up in the mountains and the frigid water made the hot ground sweat with steam.

I was exhilarated. Never before had I been so sure of what I was to do, and so confident that I would have the power to do it. There were a few patches of grass near me, and though I should have been hungry, I wasn't interested. Doing the will of the White One was my food, and I felt satisfied.

The only question that remained was the route of escape. For an instant my horse sense said, "back from where we came." That voice, however, was quickly drowned out by the remembered voice of the dark horse. *"The White One never leads us back—only forward. He will provide a way."*

Moving on upstream, I found what I supposed to be that ledge on the wall that the mare had called "Death Walk." It looked easy. Too easy. I decided to examine it.

The first thing I noticed, as I climbed a few steps up the ledge, was that it wasn't natural. It was a built thing, a man-thing, and that alone made me want to shy back from it. I also saw that it appeared to lead all the way to the top. It seemed so desirable . . . and then it seemed so wrong. My perception told me the top was within easy reach, but my mind told me it couldn't possibly be that close. There was an evil mirage at work here. I began to realize that the horses whose bones littered the canyon floor were not the daring ones at all, as I had earlier supposed. They were the gullible ones, horses easily deceived.

So I backed down this death ramp, convinced that the light of the White One at night would reveal the truth about this place. But even as I backed away, I felt the grip of the illusion. The wind whispered among the rocks and I felt an urge to bolt forward—up the ledge. Surely it was only a few simple steps to the top. Up and over. Surely . . . I shook myself. Perhaps there *was* magic in this place. But it was a magic of death.

Picking my way further upstream, the thundering rush of the waterfall filled my ears. It was a magnificent falls, throwing itself from the top with such force that it hit the valley floor quite a distance away from the wall. Behind the falls, the canyon walls were still separated at the base, making me believe that at one time there was a gorge at this end of the valley much like the gorge at the opposite end where we had entered. Apparently, ancient movements of the earth had pinched this gorge closed at the top, leaving what appeared to be a tall cave behind the falls. Looking closer, I caught a glimpse of a large pool of water covering the foot of the cave. It was set back into the rock at a slightly higher level and seemed unaffected by the churning water of the falls. The pool was dark and calm. I marvelled that such tranquility could be hidden behind the menacing face of the falls. There had to be another water source than the falls itself. An underground stream, possibly? It was definitely worth investigating, but a quick glance at the low sun told me it would have to wait.

I returned to find the other horses where I had left them. The stallion stood straight and proud, watching my approach.

"Are you coming with me?" I asked him.

"No," he said, "I am not. But I will not prevent any who wish to. This is my home, this is what I have always known, and this is where I will stay."

I stood there looking at him, feeling helpless. There was nothing more I could do, nothing more I could say. I turned to the others. With a confidence that surprised myself, I cried out, *"If you would follow the White One, follow me!"* Spinning around, I took off at full gallop back across the stream and out towards the wall called Death Walk.

Even though it was twilight, I could see the landscape with greater clarity than ever before. I hadn't looked back yet, but it sounded like the group behind me was small. A horse right on my tail, maybe two or three more further back. It wasn't until we were well out of range of the others that I glanced back. The mare was running hard off my right side, steadily gaining ground. Her splendid head stretched forward on her graceful neck and a strong, steady light burned in her eyes. And when our eyes met, they seemed to burn brighter still.

After a brief run, I slowed our party down to a walk. It was not completely dark yet and there was no telling how much energy we would need for the night ahead. The air was cooler now, and a thin fog settled in on the valley floor. The other horses that had come with us were young stallions—three of them. Unlike the mare, no light shone in their eyes. Had they really made their decision yet? Were they following more out of desire . . . or fear? Perhaps they were trying to escape death in the valley, without ever placing any faith in the White One . . . at least not yet. The flash in the mare's eyes, however, cut through the fog and convinced me that she had not only trusted me, but the White One within me.

"Tell me more about your legend of the dark horse," I asked her as we walked. The story had confused me.

"There isn't much to tell," she said. "It's been so long since my father died. All I remember is that the hero of the story was a black stallion and he was a deliverer."

"But what made you think that story might relate to me? I am not a dark horse, but I did follow a dark horse into this valley. Perhaps the prophecy is about him—but—how would you know about him?"

Suddenly I realized I was talking to myself. The mare had frozen somewhere during my last comments and I looked back to see her standing there with a most quizzical look on her face.

"What do you mean, you are not the dark horse? Do you not know yourself?"

At that I looked down at my white leg, expecting to see it reflect up at me as it always did at night. But all I saw was the faint outline of a leg, hardly visible in the approaching night. I stamped it, thinking it was caked with mud. I tried scratching it with my nose. Suddenly, with a combined sense of amazement, joy, and humility, I realized what had happened. I had been singed by the fire! I was as black as this burned-out valley! I, too, was a dark horse.

And then I laughed. I threw back my head and let out a whinny so loud it startled my new companions and bounced around the canyon walls.

"What?" she exclaimed. "What is it?"

I shook my head. "Some day I will tell you the whole story. I simply am not the horse I used to be. And I am glad of it."

We continued on until we reached the wall where the "Death Walk" began, but we had difficulty finding it. Finally one of the stallions, searching in the light of the early moon, found the place where the ledge began its ascent.

The mare and I reached the spot where the young stallion was standing. Looking up the ledge through the eyes of the White One, we saw the truth. The trail went a short distance and then disappeared into the face of the canyon wall.

"This is why we travel at night," I said. "In the daylight this fine broad ledge seems to run all the way to the top. Just when you feel you're drawing close to your goal you're actually running out of road. A hoofbeat from death. I was here this afternoon, on the ledge. With a few more steps I would have added my bones to those of your friends on the valley floor."

I felt the impatience growing within me. "This is no exit at all. It's a trap. Come, follow me."

With that, I took off at a run for the waterfall. When we got there, I knew just what to do.

"Wait here," I said to the others. "There may be another way—an escape route behind the falls."

"There's Black Magic behind those falls!" squealed one of the stallions.

"The White One is stronger than any magic. Where he leads, we have nothing to fear."

"I'm coming with you," said the mare. "I don't want to miss anything."

"Your faith is eager. I like that. But it's best for you to stay. The others need your eyes just now . . . until they begin to see. Without either one of us here, they might talk themselves into going back."

"All right." She was disappointed. Almost trembling with hunger for adventure.

I crossed to the other side of the stream and followed the canyon wall in the direction of the falls. The space between the stream and the wall got thinner and thinner until I ran out of land and was standing at the edge of the falls—now a translucent curtain between me and the moon. Somehow, I had to find a way to get higher up and behind the falls to find the pool I had seen earlier. The going was slippery with spray but I soon came to a spot where I stood two legs above the pool.

I had never jumped into water before. I wasn't even sure it was deep enough. If it was not, the impact would most certainly break my legs. I looked back at the falls for a moment, watching the moon dance behind its water curtain. The pool was black, touched with silver moon-light. Surely it was deep enough. I called to the White One for help and jumped.

It was deep enough. And strangely warm. There must have been a hot spring feeding this pool. As I swam further into the earth I marveled at how the White One led me. I had peered into caves before and found them to be blacker than any night. But here there was a dim blue glow that seemed to come from the rocks themselves—as if they had been ordered to cooperate with our escape. The glow moved along with me until the water turned shallow and the cavern narrowed into a tunnel. Confident that this was a passageway formed by an underground stream, I turned and swam back for the others. Our only hope now was that it remained passable for a horse and that it would lead us out. But that we would have to find out to-gether.

Bursting out of the pool and away from the falls, I immediately sensed danger. I could hear sounds of a great commotion—even over the cascading water.

I saw them before they saw me and it looked like my mare was getting her wish for adventure. The lead stallion and his small herd had sought us out and were trying to "persuade" the mare and young stallions to stay. Appar-ently they had succeeded with one of the stallions. Only two stood with the mare, but a faint light flickered in their eyes . . . they had made their decisions. Good. The odds against us were impossible, but if it came to a fight, it was good to know who stood with the White One.

The lead stallion moved in on the mare, head low and weaving, snake-like, side to side. He was trying to herd her back into his harem, and she was fighting him with everything she had. Dodging and kicking, she landed a telling blow to his side just as the two stallions lurched in to cut him off. Me? I'd seen enough. I ran straight for the lead stallion. He heard me coming, and stood his ground, waiting.

"What's going on here?" I demanded. "You said these horses were free to go."

"The foolish stallions may run where they will. I did not mean that my favorite mare was free to kill herself following a mad horse."

His flaring nostrils and flapping ears warned me he was ready to lunge. I spoke quietly.

"So now you are going back on your own word. The honor of a lead stallion means no more than this to you?"

"You lie. I am merely trying to persuade her to stay—for her own good."

"That was certainly a lot more than persuasion I saw going on," I said, positioning myself between him and the mare. Without taking my eyes from him, I called back to her. "Lead the stallions across the stream to the pool behind the falls. Follow it into the mountain and I will catch up with you."

As they broke for the stream behind me, the stallion shouted at them:

"There's Black Magic behind that falls!"

"I am beginning to wonder," I said, clearly and loudly for all to hear, "if it is Black Magic or *your* magic that is keeping these horses in captivity here."

At that he went for me.

Now I am not a fighter. I'd lived a sheltered ranchhorse life and my only fighting experience was for play—the usual high-spirited stallion stuff. I felt totally unprepared for an encounter with an enraged, battle-scarred range horse.

There would have been no chance for me at all in daylight. But at night . . . the light of the White One filled my eyes and I could see him much easier than he could see me. A choice advantage. I was fighting a wild stallion, but he was fighting a stallion and the night.

It was during this fight I realized something astonishing: Those who don't believe in the White One cannot see the light in our eyes. If he had seen the twin flames of my eyes, he would have had a target. As it was, most of his slicing kicks and vicious bites just missed my twisting, turning body.

I had no desire to hurt or cripple the proud stallion. I didn't want to win or lose. My whole desire was to give the others time to flee—and then look for my own chance to escape. That chance came when I caught him rearing. He wanted to slash down on me with his front hooves—but he never got the chance. Instead, I suddenly lunged my whole weight against the side of his belly.

The timing was perfect. Caught completely by surprise, his legs flew out from beneath him. For a moment, he seemed suspended in mid-air. Then came a sickening thud and the loud grunt of air that smashed from his lungs as he hit the rock-hard soil.

The stallion's fall gave me the chance I'd been waiting for. With the blood pounding in my head, and a warm flow of it trickling into my eyes, I ran for the falls. I knew that once I hit the pool I would be safe. The stallion would not violate his own warning of "Black Magic."

Looking behind me, I could see him pursuing, but too far back to be of any concern. I found myself feeling glad he was not hurt and genuinely sorry for him. The real "magic" was pride. Pride that kept him prisoner in a valley of ashes. Pride that fed his dominance over the weaker ones who ran in his trail.

With a flying leap, I plunged once more into the dark waters of the pool. Its warmth enveloped me, bathing my wounds and calming my racing heart for the tedious crawl through the tunnel.

Once again, the strange, sourceless light led me. As I picked my way along, I noticed the eerie beauty of this watery shaft. There were pointed spines of rock hanging from the ceiling, and others, like seedlings of stone, that seemed to sprout up from the cave floor. Still others, I could tell, had made complete columns from top to bottom. No more. Like so many weathered corral planks, they had been kicked aside by the fleeing horses in front of me. And in my mind's eye I could imagine the mare smashing her way through this cavern, leading her friends to freedom. What a queen among horses! She had jumped into following the White One with everything she had, and I loved her.

Just when I was beginning to wonder why I hadn't caught up with them yet, I noticed that the dim light had seemed to focus in countless glowing points. Then with a start I realized I was looking into the star-washed night through a cave opening.

Stumbling out into the cold night air, I was immediately rushed upon by five excited horses. The mare was licking the blood away from a tear in my ear. Then she walked around me, looking me over with a quick appraising gaze. "You have a gash on your hip," she said, "but it will heal. A few cuts and scratches. You'll be fine. You are a brave one, aren't you? Tell me what happened."

"The White One gave me light," I said. "I was able to catch the stallion off balance and put him on his side long enough to make my break."

"Is he all right?" she asked.

"Yes. He ran after me, but mostly for show, I think. He had no intention of following."

"He is such a prideful horse," she said with pity, "and to think that all along we were just a short trip away from freedom."

"Who are these other horses?" I asked.

"They are two mares who slipped away during the fight."

One of them spoke up. "When you said it was the stallion and not the magic that was keeping us there it all made sense."

I was overjoyed. My conflict had played a part in freeing two more horses.

"And the young stallions?" I asked.

"Two of us are here," said one. "The other *wanted* to come, I think—but he couldn't overcome the power of the lead stallion."

"Our fear has turned into purpose," said his friend. "We want to go back and free the others . . . show them how easy it is to get out."

"That is a good sign," I said, "but you must run with us for a season and learn from the White One. It is not as easy as you think."

I paused for a moment, delighting in the strong, steady light that burned in all their eyes. "I want all of you to mark this spot. It is a place to remember; a place of your first faith in the White One. Soon you may be returning to free your brothers and sisters. Perhaps they will listen to you."

My mare broke into these thoughts with a firm urgency that made us all straighten up.

"I have checked out our position," she said. "As you can see, we have emerged from the underground stream fed by the lake in front of us here. On the other side of the lake is a relatively short, rocky descent to the foothills.

From there we can once again pick up the river that comes from out of the mountains. I saw its reflection in the moonlight. I think we should run the river until dawn and take shelter where we can."

I stood staring at her, in spite of myself. Adventure danced in her eyes and her graceful forehooves pawed the ground with impatience. I could only shake my head in wonder.

"Lead on, brave mare!"

I stood for a moment, and watched them leap across the rocks and dash to the far side of the lake. I watched them drop out of sight, one by one, in their descent to the foothills. And I waited until I saw them reappear on the smooth ground below me, their eyes now pinneedles of light. One, two, three, four, five racing silhouettes, galloping hard and free in the joy of the White One.

Then, with a loud whinny to no one in particular, I lifted my forelegs to the starry sky and set off to join them.

For further information on John Fischer contact:
Tom Willet, Artist Management, P.O. Box 50590, Nashville, TN 37205,
(615) 269-9966.